LEVERS & PULLEYS

by
Alex Brinded

©2018
Book Life
King's Lynn
Norfolk PE30 4LS

ISBN: 978-1-78637-307-6

All rights reserved
Printed in Malaysia

Written by:
Alex Brinded

Edited by:
Holly Duhig

Designed by:
Gareth Liddington

A catalogue record for this book is available from the British Library.

Photocredits: Abbreviations: l-left, r-right, b-bottom, t-top, c-centre, m-middle. All images are courtesy of Shutterstock.com.
Cover – Jenn Huls, Dorothy Chiron, Sicco Hesselmans, levente imre takacs, espies, Olesia Bilkei, a_v_d, donatas1205, snapper8S8, Ljupco Smokovski, 2 – SUMITH NUNKHAM, 4 – Robert Kneschke, 5 – haveseen, 6 – Catalin Petolea, 7 – Steve Norman, 8 – Alexey Pevnev, Warren Chan, 9 – humbak, 10 – Marko Aliaksandr, zlikovec, 11 – travelpeter, Kingtony, 12 – Dirk M. de Boer, 13 – Photobac, 14 – wandee007, 15 – fizkes, 16 – PHILIPIMAGE, 17 – wavebreakmedia, 18 – Monkey Business Images, 19 – mik ulyannikov, 20 – s_oleg, 21 – Irene Kripa, 22 – Syda Productions, 23 – Ekaterina_Minaeva, 24 – Hamdyzainal.

Images are courtesy of Shutterstock.com. With thanks to Getty Images, Thinkstock Photo and iStockphoto.

All facts, statistics, web addresses and URLs in this book were verified as valid and accurate at time of writing. No responsibility for any changes to external websites or references can be accepted by either the author or publisher.

CONTENTS

Page 4   Working Hard
Page 6   What Is a Pulley?
Page 8   Motorised Pulleys
Page 10 Cranes
Page 12 Pulling Tight
Page 14 Conveyor Belts
Page 16 What Is a Lever?
Page 18 Seesaws
Page 20 Levers as Tools
Page 22 Door Handles
Page 23 Levers as Brakes
Page 24 Glossary and Index

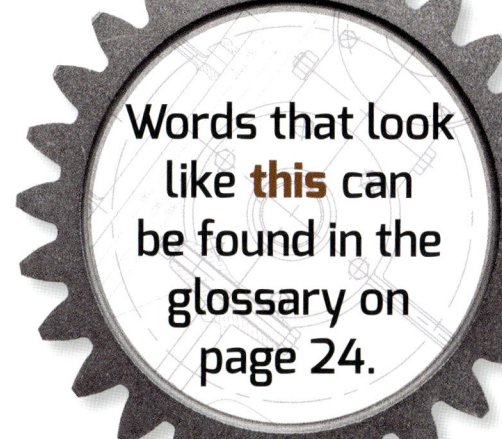

Words that look like **this** can be found in the glossary on page 24.

WORKING HARD

Moving something heavy can be hard work. Luckily, there are lots of machines we can use to make pushing, pulling and lifting a lot easier.

Friends can help if they are nearby!

This chair lift has a giant pulley to take skiers up a mountain.

Pulleys and levers help us to move big loads or heavy objects. Using a pulley or lever makes the load feel much lighter!

5

WHAT IS A PULLEY?

This boy is getting water from a well with a pulley.

A pulley is a simple device made by wrapping a rope or a belt around a wheel. It can be used for easily lifting and lowering heavy objects.

A pulley system has a loop of rope wrapped around two or more wheels. The load feels lighter each time the rope is wrapped around the wheels.

The rope is wrapped around this pulley system three times.

MOTORISED PULLEYS

A pulley that is powered by a motor is called a motorised pulley. The motor makes the drive wheel turn.

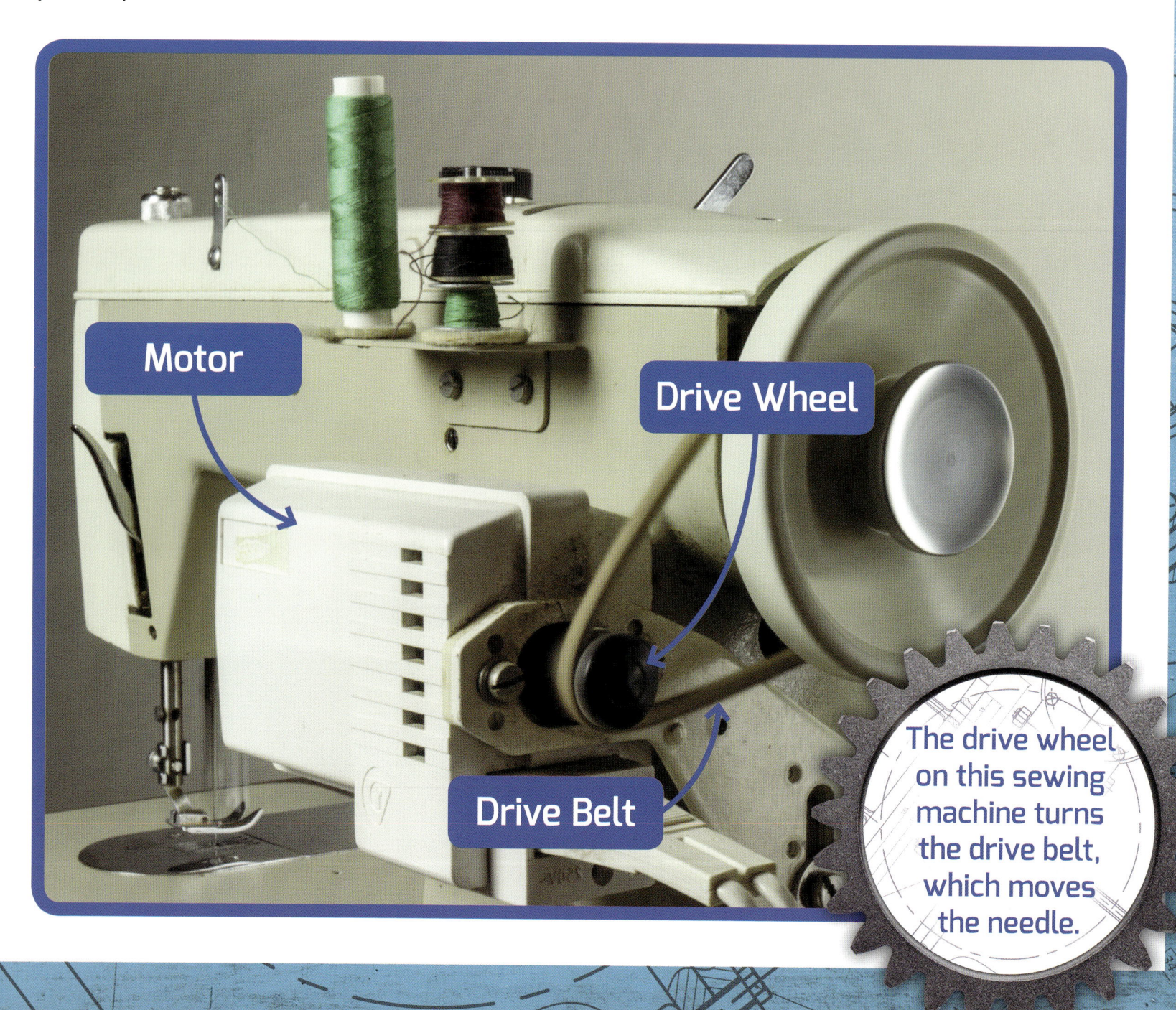

Motor

Drive Wheel

Drive Belt

The drive wheel on this sewing machine turns the drive belt, which moves the needle.

A **motor** with a pulley system moves this elevator up and down. The steel cable is **wound** in to lift the elevator, and **unwound** to lower it.

CRANES

These giant cranes move huge amounts of earth.

Sheave

Crane Arm

The sheaves have grooves in so the cable doesn't slip off.

Cranes are big machines that use motorised pulleys. They lift heavy loads upwards and side to side. Cranes use wheels called sheaves.

Cranes usually have two sheaves. One sheave is attached to the hook and the other is attached to the crane arm.

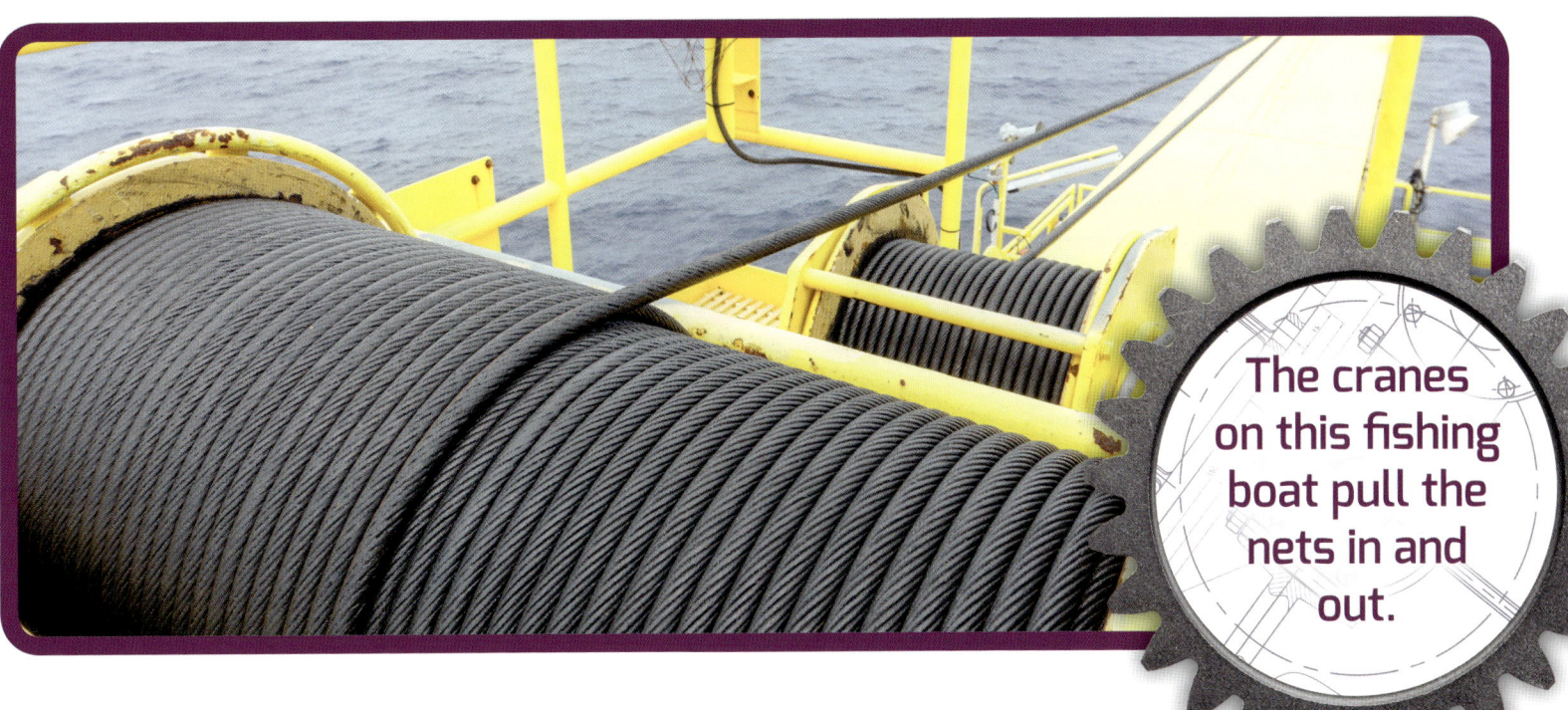

The cranes on this fishing boat pull the nets in and out.

PULLING TIGHT

Pulleys can be used to hold **tension**. Parts of a boat, like a sail, need to be moved when changing direction but then held tightly in place after.

By using pulleys, these ropes can be pulled very tight by hand and loosened quickly.

The buddy pulls in the rope as the climber goes up to keep it under tension.

Rock climbers use pulleys for safety. The pulley makes it easy for a climbing buddy to prevent a climber from falling if they slip. This is called belaying.

CONVEYOR BELTS

The conveyor belt in this mine moves rocks out of the pit.

A conveyor belt, like one at a supermarket, is a pulley. A wide belt is looped round big rollers. Conveyor belts can carry lots of things over a short distance and be **automated**.

A luggage carousel is a huge conveyor belt used in airports. The wide rubber belt carries the luggage from outside the airport, near the **runway**, to the passengers inside.

Luggage carousels are a fast way of getting all the passengers' bags off the plane.

WHAT IS A LEVER?

Levers, like pulleys, are also used to make a job easier. They are made from a **pivot** and a rod. The pivot is fixed and doesn't move. You can move the rod to move the object.

In this picture, the screwdriver is the rod. It pivots on the edge of the paint pot to open the lid.

Pivot Point

A wheelbarrow makes it easier to move loads; even children!

A wheelbarrow is a lever with a pivot point at the front. When the handles are lifted, the wheel stays on the ground and can be pushed forwards.

SEESAWS

A seesaw is a fun lever that has a pivot point in the middle. The heavier end will go down whilst the lighter end will go up in the air.

By pushing with your legs you can add force to push one end of the see saw up. If both ends have the same weight on them, the seesaw will be balanced and horizontal.

This girl has one foot either side of the pivot point, so the see-saw is balanced.

LEVERS AS TOOLS

Scissors are levers. The pivot point is where the two blades are attached, just above the handles. Opening and closing the handles makes the blades cut through things.

Pivot Point

Cooking tongs are used a lot for BBQs.

Cooking tongs are also levers. They allow the chef to move food whilst it is being cooked and is too hot to touch.

DOOR HANDLES

Turning the handle moves the door latch so the door can be opened.

Door handles are small levers that turn a latch. When a door is closed, a metal latch slots into a hole in the doorframe. When the door handle is pulled down, the latch is pulled out of the slot, allowing the door to be opened.

LEVERS AS BRAKES

Bike brakes are levers that pull a brake wire. As the brake wire is pulled, the brakes begin to close. This slows and stops the bike.

By squeezing the brakes lightly, the whole bike can be slowed a lot.

GLOSSARY

automated — a machine that works on its own
balanced — when something is steady and level
motor — a motor is a device that turns electricity into movement
pivot — a point where something can rotate, swing or move side to side
runway — a wide, long strip on which aircraft take off and land
tension — when something has been stretched and is held tight
unwound — to unwind something completely
wound — to wind something in completely

INDEX

belt 6, 9, 14-15
rope 6-7, 12-13
wheels 6-7, 9-10, 17
cable 8, 10
turn 9, 22
work 4
load 7, 10, 17
weight 19